MARGARITA

Anglican Prayer Beads

PRAYER FOR
JOYFUL JOURNEYS

"*Remember,*
you are free to pray the rosary
in any way you wish.
It is a private devotion."

Pope John Paul II
Rosarium Virginis Mariae, 2002

Inspired by

Mary, our Blessed Mother and
dedicated to my favorite women:

DAUGHTERS AND GRANDDAUGHTERS

Jess Ennis and Kate Gurri Glass,
Taryn and Kaitlyn Ennis
the joys of my life;

MOTHER, FRIENDS AND SISTER

Beba Gurri, Jean Glass, Sister Rita Baum, Janice Wetter
Jane Stapp, Jean Jeakle, Margaret Mullane and
Irene Gurri, for simple prayers and simple faith;

and

most of all, to my twin,
Elena Gurri Levis,
the wisest and funniest woman I know!

OTHER BOOKS BY AUTHOR:
The Trilogy of Anger

ISBN: 978-0-615-78217-1
LCCN:

MARGARITA GURRI, PH.D.

P.O. Box 1806, Dania Beach, FL 33004
Email: Margarita@DrGurri.com
www.facebook.com/margarita.gurri
www.DrMargaritaGurri.com
954-609-9904

Designed by Caley Curchy, Edited by Steve Lee

Anglican Prayer Beads

PRAYER FOR
JOYFUL JOURNEYS

Table of Contents

* Note: Anglican Prayer Beads is a booklet made from excerpts taken from my Little Prayer Bead Booklet (Gurri unpublished draft) to share with the women at the Joyful Journeys Women's Retreat, St. Thomas Episcopal Church, Coral Gables, FL at the Duncan Center, Delray, FL, March 2004, 2nd printing March 2008, 3rd November 2008, 4th December ©2009, 5th May 2011.

"*Faith*
is simple,
not easy."

Margarita Gurri. Ph.D.

Anglican Prayer Beads

INTRODUCTION

I WAS, and am, awed by the power of beautiful beads that bring peace to so many faces and kneeling forms.

"My first rosary was made of big, rough, blue plastic beads with a big, white plastic crucifix. I kept this rosary until someone needed it more."

Preparing for the Joyful Journeys Women's Retreat rosary-making workshop for St. Thomas Episcopal Church, Coral Gables, FL continues to remind me of the good in the world and of the power of prayer. Faith is simple, not easy. Faith, as taught to me by my Roman Catholic mother, the late Beba Gurri, is practical and alive. The rosary connects us all to God, to each other and to grace. The rosary is a time-honored pathway to prayer.

"Simple prayer, simple faith"

These words are borrowed from my friend, Jean Jeakle. After much research, scouring of books, articles, the internet and several knowledgeable humans, I amused myself with my efforts to look beyond the simple, basic truths. Here are some basic truths affirmed in my prayerful journey. Like most joyful journeys, it has been worth the struggle and messiness.

- "Simple prayers, simple faith (Jean Jeakle).
- Prayer is a response to God, "by thought and by deeds, with or without words" (Episcopal Church's Book of Common Prayer, BCP).
- We pray because "God told us to pray" (Anonymous meditant).
- "We pray with beads, ropes or ties to keep count (Anon).
- "We pray to talk to God (Anon).
- "We pray the rosary because Mary told us to" (Anon).
- We pray to listen to God. "The purpose of real prayer is to be still enough to allow God to speak to us, to allow ourselves to meditate, so that through meditation, we hope that God speaks to each of us" (the Rt. Rev. Monsignor D.A. Provino, Orthodox Catholic priest).
- We pray for peace and goodness in our world.

Anglican Prayer Beads

THE ROSARY

The Rosary

THE EARLIEST document I have found citing the use of a prayer device stems from the 300s A.D. It is comforting to continue the cycle of prayer begun with fingers, berries, pebbles, knots, loose beads, strung prayer beads, chaplets, rosaries, and, more recently, tattoos, used as prayer counters. What a striking miracle that these basic physical objects become sacramental when blessed (BCP). Anglican Prayer Beads is a work in progress intended to introduce a historical and daily context for these prayer beads.

In the Middle Ages, strung prayer beads varied in length because they represented the number of penances undertaken by the meditant. The penance was often the Our Father and so the strung prayer beads came to be known as Pater Nosters or prayer counters. Later, when the Marian (pertaining to Mary) prayer beads came into being, Hail Marys replaced the Our Fathers, but the custom of calling them Pater Nosters continued. In the Roman Catholic tradition, the strung prayer beads representing the 15 mysteries of the life of Jesus Christ were called The Rosary. In time, the Dominican Rosary retained the name, even though it contained only one third of the beads, representing just five mysteries. Chaplets refer to strung prayer beads devoted to the saints, particular religious orders and devotion. Over time, the term rosary became generic for strung bead prayer.

About the Anglican or Episcopal Rosary

The Episcopal Rosary is a relatively new prayer tool. It was born in the 1980s of a decade-long contemplative prayer group led by an Episcopal priest. The group's mission was to foster contemplative prayer by "bringing into use the whole of us--body, mind and spirit" (Solitaries of DeKoven 4). The Anglican Rosary is a blending of the traditions of the Roman Catholic or Marian Rosary and the Orthodox Jesus Prayer Rope.

As with more ancient prayer beads, pebbles, stones and knots, the Anglican Rosary is a prayer counter. The rosary is steeped in theology and symbolism that affirms the Celtic view of the sanctity of all of God's creation.

Structure of the Anglican Rosary

The Anglican Rosary was created with 33 beads, one for every year Jesus Christ served on earth (please see page 8).

- Four groups of seven beads form the Weeks and reminds us of Creation, the temporal week … and the seasons.
- The number seven signifies wholeness or completion (Solitaries 4).
- The four cruciform beads "remind us that the Cross is the central symbol of our Christian Anglican faith … of the seasons of the temporal year, and the four points on the compass, thus bringing us into mindfulness of the created world." (Solitaries 3)

Anglican Prayer Beads

Anglican Prayer Bracelet or Chaplet

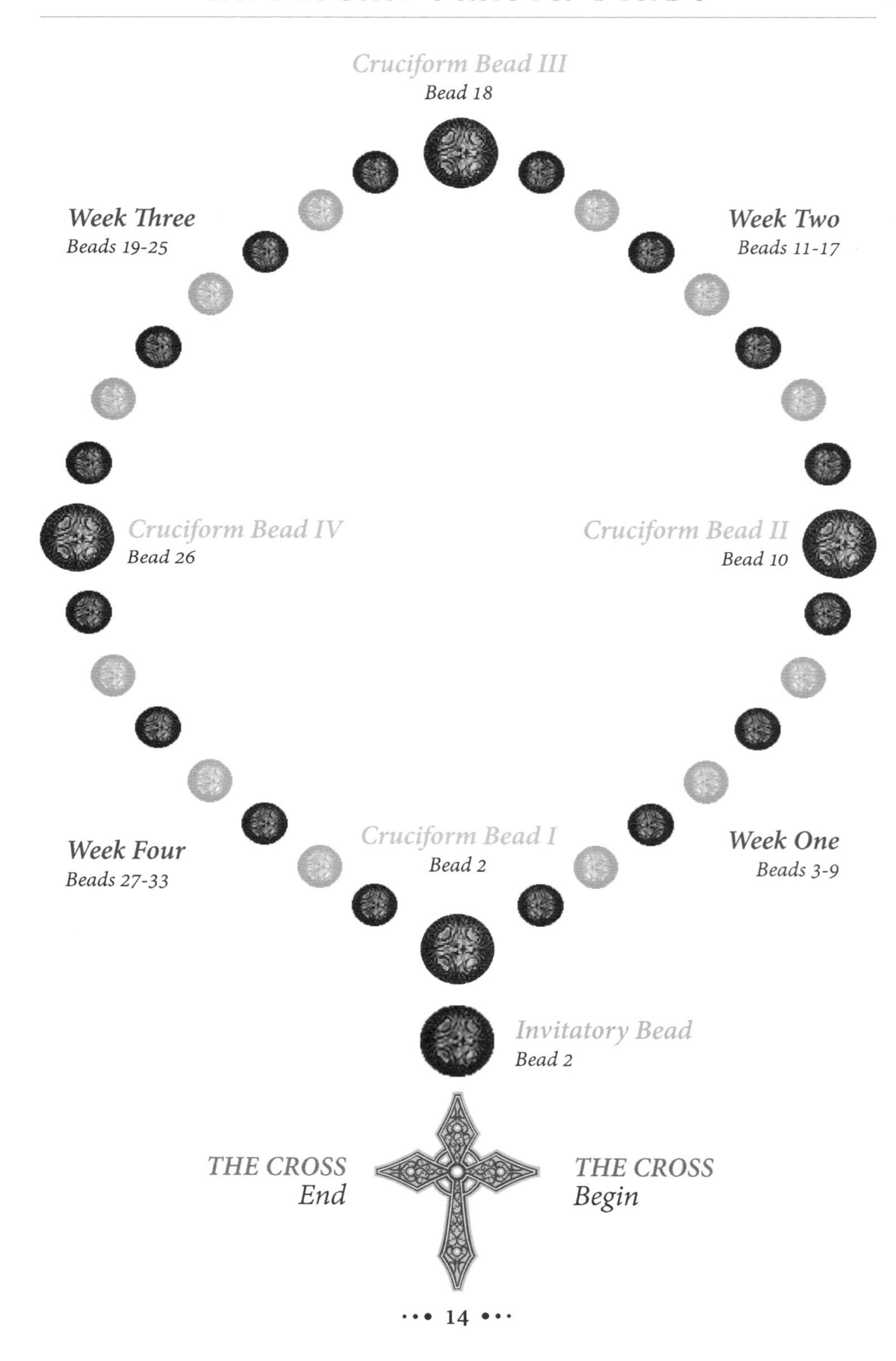
Cruciform Bead III
Bead 18
Week Three
Beads 19-25
Week Two
Beads 11-17
Cruciform Bead IV
Bead 26
Cruciform Bead II
Bead 10
Week Four
Beads 27-33
Cruciform Bead I
Bead 2
Week One
Beads 3-9
Invitatory Bead
Bead 2
THE CROSS
End
THE CROSS
Begin

Anglican Prayer Beads

PRAYING THE ROSARY

"Pray the rosary,
and any prayer, anyway, anytime,
anywhere … Any prayer is wonderful."

Father Del Provino

Praying the Rosary

WHILE IT can be helpful to share a prayer ritual with precise words with others in a faith community, there is no right way to pray. This is true for the rosary.

- "We pray for the intercession of Mary and all the saints. We can pray directly but why not get all the help we can get." (Father Del Provino)
- The most important thing about the rosary is prayer. Anonymous
- Praying the rosary is a re-telling of the life of Jesus Christ, divided into the Joyful, the Sorrowful, the Glorious and the Luminous Mysteries. It is a contemplative tool.

Prayerful Attitude

My favorite Roman Catholic nun, Sister Rita Baum, formerly Sister Paul Joseph, taught me to pray the rosary. My mother taught me to love it as an everyday practice.

- From a busy mother of four, I learned to start the day by praying the rosary, in my head, once my feet hit the floor. Hardly a contemplative approach, this method has struck a chord with many a focused, active and busy person.
- Having a rosary, even if never actively prayed, connects each of us to the grace of prayer in our world.
- Carrying the rosary, holding the rosary, or even thinking about the rosary is a tactile connection to the sacred.

Anglican Rosary Prayers

In keeping with the Anglican tradition, **the Anglican Rosary invites prayer inspired by the individual meditant.** Each meditant prays to the moment, the need, open to the Holy Spirit.

As a reference point, I present some prayer forms created and used by other Episcopalians.

- All of the prayer forms I have discovered begin and end with the Cross and Sign of the Cross.
- For the sake of clarity, I have numbered and labeled the path to prayer for several prayer forms found in a little folded-paper booklet found in the Trinity Cathedral Bookstore, Miami, FL. I thank the Anonymous author.
- Most prayers are taken from the Book of Common Prayer (BCP).

Basic Rhythm of the Anglican Rosary Prayers

The rosary is prayed in a fluid path, beginning with the Cross, then the Invitatory Bead, praying the entire bead loop and meditating a final time on the Invitatory Bead and the Cross.

- **The rosary begins with a blessing and a note of thanks.**
- **The Cross** invites the beginning and the end of the prayers, saying the Sign of the Cross.
- **The Invitatory Bead** sets the theme of the prayers.
- **The Cruciform Beads** invite the same prayers for the four beads that separate the Week Beads.
- **Week Beads** vary in inviting the same or different prayers for each of the seven-bead groups of the four weeks.
- **A** Glory Be is invited after each of the **Week** Beads.
- The repeated, final **Invitatory Bead**, or Collect, invites the Lord's Prayer.
- **The rosary ends with a blessing and a note of thanks.**

Basic Template of the Anglican Rosary Prayers

Below is a basic template of the Anglican Rosary Prayers suggested by an anonymous meditant. I have highlighted the Cruciform Beads for clarity and to reinforce their symbolic meanings and separation of the Weeks.

BEAD	NAME OF BEAD	PRAYER
Begin	**The Cross**	• *Sign of the Cross*
1	**Invitatory Bead**	• *Sets the theme of the rosary prayers*
2	**Cruciform Bead I**	• *Summation and contemplation for petitions*
3-9	**Week One**	• *Specific intentions or petitions* • *Glory Be*
10	**Cruciform Bead II**	• *Summation and contemplation for petitions*
11-17	**Week Two**	• *Specific intentions or petitions* • *Glory Be*
18	**Cruciform Bead III**	• *Summation and contemplation for petitions*
19-25	**Week Three**	• *Specific intentions or petitions* • *Glory Be*
26	**Cruciform Bead IV**	• *Summation and contemplation for petitions*
27-33	**Week Four**	• *Specific intentions or petitions* • *Glory Be*
End	**Cruciform Bead I**	• *Lord's Prayer*
End	**Invitatory Bead**	• *Collect*
End	**Cross**	• *Let us bless the Lord* • *Thanks be to God* • *Sign of the Cross*

PRAYERS SAID WITH ANGLICAN PRAYER BEADS

Sign of the Cross

In the name of the Father,

- *and the Son,*
- *and the Holy Spirit. Amen.*

The Glory Be (book of common prayer, bcp)

Glory be to the Father,

- *and to the Son,*
- *and to the Holy Spirit;*
- *as it was in the beginning,*
- *is now and ever shall be*
- *world without end. Amen.*

Collect

Please refer to the Book of Common Prayer (BCP) for a thoughtful selection of the Collect fitting the season, occasion and needs. Below is a traditional prayer "Of a Saint" and one of my favorite:

- *Almighty God, who by thy Holy Spirit hast made us one with thy saints in heaven and on earth:*
- *Grant that in our earthly pilgrimage we may ever be supported by this fellowship of love and prayer, and may know ourselves to be surrounded by their witness to thy power and mercy.*
- *We ask this for the sake of Jesus Christ, in whom all our intercessions are acceptable through the Spirit, and who liveth and reigneth forever and ever. Amen.*

Hail Mary (Roman Catholic prayer)

Hail Mary,
- *full of grace,*
- *The Lord is with thee;*

Blessed art thou amongst women
- *and blessed is the fruit of thy womb, Jesus.*

Son of Mary, Son of the Living God,
- *have mercy upon us sinners,*
- *now, and at the hour of our death. Amen.*

The Lord's Prayer (BCP 121)

Our Father, who art in heaven,
- *hallowed be Thy Name,*
- *Thy kingdom come,*
- *Thy will be done,*
- *on earth as it is in heaven.*

Give us this day our daily bread.
And forgive us our trespasses,
- *as we forgive those who trespass against us.*

And lead us not unto temptation,
- *but deliver us from evil.*

For thine is the kingdom,
- *and the power,*
- *and the glory,*
- *forever and ever. Amen.*

The Apostles' Creed (BCP 398)

I believe in God, the Father almighty,

- *Creator of heaven and earth.*

I believe in Jesus Christ, his only Son, our Lord.

- *He was conceived by the power of the Holy Spirit and born of the Virgin Mary.*
- *He suffered under Pontius Pilate,*
- *was crucified, died and was buried.*
- *He descended to the dead.*
- *On the third day He rose again.*
- *He ascended into heaven,*
- *and is seated at the right hand of the Father.*
- *He will come again to judge the living and the dead.*

I believe in the Holy Spirit,

- *the holy Catholic Church,*
- *the communion of saints,*
- *the forgiveness of sins,*
- *the resurrection of the body and the life everlasting. Amen.*

Magnificat, The Song of Mary, Luke 1:46-55 (BCP 119)

My soul proclaims the greatness of the Lord,

- *my spirit rejoices in God my Savior;*

For He has looked with favor on his lowly servant,
From this day all generations will call me blessed;

- *the Almighty has done great things for me,*
- *and holy is His Name.*

He has mercy on those who fear Him in every generation.
He has shown the strength of His arm,

- *He has scattered the proud in their conceit.*

He has cast down the mighty from their thrones,

- *and has lifted up the lowly.*

He has filled the hungry with good things,

- *and the rich He has sent away empty.*

He has come to the help of His servant, Israel,

- *for He has remembered His promise of mercy,*

The promise He made to our fathers,

- *to Abraham and his children forever.*

Glory to the Father

Glory to the Father,
and to the Son,

- *and to the Holy Spirit:*
- *as it was*
- *in the beginning,*
- *is now, and ever shall be*
- *world without end. Amen.*

"The winds of grace are always blowing ... but it is you that must raise your sails."

Rabinadanath Tagore

A Morning Devotion

BEAD	NAME OF BEAD	PRAYER
Begin	The Cross	· *Sign of the Cross*
1	Invitatory Bead	· *Lord, open our lips, and our mouth shall proclaim Your praise.* · *Glory Be*
2	Cruciform Bead I	***Open my lips, O God, and my mouth shall proclaim Your praise.***
3-9	Week One	· *To You I lift up my soul; my God, I put my trust in You.* · *Glory Be*
10	Cruciform Bead II	***Cast me not away from Your presence and take not Your Holy Spirit from me.***
11-17	Week Two	· *To You I lift up my soul; my God, I put my trust in You.* · *Glory Be*
18	Cruciform Bead III	***Cast me not away from Your presence and take not Your Holy Spirit from me.***
19-25	Week Three	· *To You I lift up my soul; my God, I put my trust in You.* · *Glory Be*
26	Cruciform Bead IV	***Cast me not away from Your presence and take not Your Holy Spirit from me.***
27-33	Week Four	· *To You I lift up my soul; my God, I put my trust in You.* · *Glory Be*
End	Cruciform Bead I	· *The Lord's Prayer*
End	Ending Invitatory Bead (Collect)	***Lord God, almighty and everlasting Father, You have brought us Your mighty power, that we may not fall into sin, nor be overcome by adversity; and in all we do, direct us to the fulfilling of Your purpose; through Jesus Christ our Lord. Amen***
End	Cross	· *Let us bless the Lord* · *Thanks be to God* · *Sign of the Cross*

An Evening Devotion

BEAD	NAME OF BEAD	PRAYER
Begin	The Cross	• *Sign of the Cross*
1	Invitatory Bead	• *O God, make speed to save us. O Lord, make haste to help us.* • *Glory Be*
2	Cruciform Bead I	***Let the Name of the Lord be blessed, from this time forth forevermore. From the rising of the sun to its going down, let the Name of the Lord be praised.***
3-9	Week One	• *You, O Lord, are my lamp; my God, You make my darkness bright.* • *Glory Be*
10	Cruciform Bead II	***Create in me a clean heart, O God, and renew a right spirit within me.***
11-17	Week Two	• *You, O Lord, are my lamp; my God, You make my darkness bright.* • *Glory Be*
18	Cruciform Bead III	***Cast me not away from Your presence and take not Your Holy Spirit from me.***
19-25	Week Three	• *You, O Lord, are my lamp; my God, You make my darkness bright.* • *Glory Be*
26	Cruciform Bead IV	***Give me the joy of Your saving help again and sustain me with Your bountiful spirit.***
27-33	Week Four	• *You, O Lord, are my lamp; my God, You make my darkness bright.* • *Glory Be*
End	Cruciform Bead I	• *The Lord's Prayer*
End	Ending Invitatory Bead (Collect)	***Lord Jesus, stay with us, for evening is at hand and the day is past; be our companion in the way. Kindle our hearts, and awaken hope, that we may know You as You are revealed in Scripture and the breaking of bread. Grant this for the sake of Your love. Amen.***
End	Cross	• *Let us bless the Lord* • *Thanks be to God* • *Sign of the Cross*

Praise and Thanksgiving

BEAD	NAME OF BEAD	PRAYER
Begin	The Cross	• *Sign of the Cross*
1	Invitatory Bead	• *O God, make speed to save us. O Lord, make haste to help us.* • *Glory Be*
2	Cruciform Bead I	***Glorify the Lord, all you works of the Lord, praise Him and highly exalt Him forever. In the firmament of His power, glorify the Lord, praise Him and highly exalt Him forever.***
3-9	Week One	• *By the word of the Lord were the heavens made, by the breath of His mouth all the heavenly hosts.* • *Glory Be*
10	Cruciform Bead II	***Glorify the Lord, all you works of the Lord, praise Him and highly exalt Him forever. In the firmament of His power, glorify the Lord, praise Him and highly exalt Him forever.***
11-17	Week Two	• *By the word of the Lord were the heavens made, by the breath of His mouth all the heavenly hosts.* • *Glory Be*
18	Cruciform Bead III	***Glorify the Lord, all you works of the Lord, praise Him and highly exalt Him forever. In the firmament of His power, glorify the Lord, praise Him and highly exalt Him forever.***
19-25	Week Three	• *By the word of the Lord were the heavens made, by the breath of His mouth all the heavenly hosts.* • *Glory Be*
26	Cruciform Bead IV	***Glorify the Lord, all you works of the Lord, praise Him and highly exalt Him forever. In the firmament of His power, glorify the Lord, praise Him and highly exalt Him forever.***
27-33	Week Four	• *By the word of the Lord were the heavens made, by the breath of His mouth all the heavenly hosts.* • *Glory Be*

BEAD	NAME OF BEAD	PRAYER
End	**Cruciform Bead I**	• *The Lord's Prayer*
End	**Ending Invitatory Bead (Collect)**	***We give You thanks, most gracious God, for the beauty of earth and sky and sea; for the richness of mountains, plains, and rivers; for the songs of birds and the loveliness of flowers. We praise You for these good gifts, and pray that we may safeguard them for our posterity. Grant that we may continue to grow in our grateful enjoyment of Your Name, now and forever. Amen.***
End	**Cross**	• *Let us bless the Lord* • *Thanks be to God* • *Sign of the Cross*

Holy Mary, Bearer of God
Have mercy on me, your sister.

Trisagion and the Jesus Prayer

BEAD	NAME OF BEAD	PRAYER
Begin	**The Cross**	• *Sign of the Cross*
1	**Invitatory Bead**	• *O God, make speed to save us. O Lord, make haste to help us.* • *Glory Be*
2	**Cruciform Bead I**	***Holy God, Holy and Mighty, Holy Immortal One, have mercy upon us.***
3-9	**Week One**	• *Lord Jesus Christ, son of the Living God, have mercy upon me, a sinner.* • *Glory Be*
10	**Cruciform Bead II**	***Holy God, Holy and Mighty, Holy Immortal One, have mercy upon us.***
11-17	**Week Two**	• *Lord Jesus Christ, son of the Living God, have mercy upon me, a sinner.* • *Glory Be*
18	**Cruciform Bead III**	***Holy God, Holy and Mighty, Holy Immortal One, have mercy upon us.***
19-25	**Week Three**	• *Lord Jesus Christ, son of the Living God, have mercy upon me, a sinner.* • *Glory Be*
26	**Cruciform Bead IV**	***Holy God, Holy and Mighty, Holy Immortal One, have mercy upon us.***
27-33	**Week Four**	• *Lord Jesus Christ, son of the Living God, have mercy upon me, a sinner.* • *Glory Be*
End	**Cruciform Bead I**	• *The Lord's Prayer*
End	**Ending Invitatory Bead (Collect)**	***"Peace I give you; My own peace I leave with you." Regard not our sins, but the faith of your Church, and give us the peace and unity of that heavenly City, where the Father and the Holy Spirit live and reign, now and forever. Amen.***
End	**Cross**	• *Let us bless the Lord* • *Thanks be to God* • *Sign of the Cross*

A Marian Devotion

BEAD	NAME OF BEAD	PRAYER
Begin	The Cross	• *Sign of the Cross*
1	Invitatory Bead	• *O God, make speed to save us. O Lord, make haste to help us.* • *Glory Be*
2	Cruciform Bead I	***The angel of the Lord announced to Mary, and she conceived by the Holy Spirit.***
3-9	Week One	• *Hail Mary* • *Glory Be*
10	Cruciform Bead II	***Behold the handmaid of the Lord; be it done to me according to Your word.***
11-17	Week Two	• *Hail Mary* • *Glory Be*
18	Cruciform Bead III	***And the Word was made flesh, and dwelt among us.***
19-25	Week Three	• *Hail Mary* • *Glory Be*
26	Cruciform Bead IV	***Pray for us, O Holy Mother of God, that we may be made worthy of the promises of Christ.***
27-33	Week Four	• *Hail Mary* • *Glory Be*
End	Cruciform Bead I	• *The Lord's Prayer*
End	Ending Invitatory Bead (Collect)	***Pour Your grace into our hearts, O Lord, that we who have known the incarnation of Your Son, Jesus Christ, announced by the angel to the Virgin Mary, may, by His cross and passion, be brought to the glory of His resurrection; who lives and reigns with You, in the unity of the Holy Spirit, one God, now and forever. Amen.***
End	Cross	• *Let us bless the Lord* • *Thanks be to God* • *Sign of the Cross*

Anglican Prayer Beads

ANCIENT ROSARY TRADITIONS

Ancient Rosary Traditions

Jesus Beads, modern version of Orthodox prayer ropes.

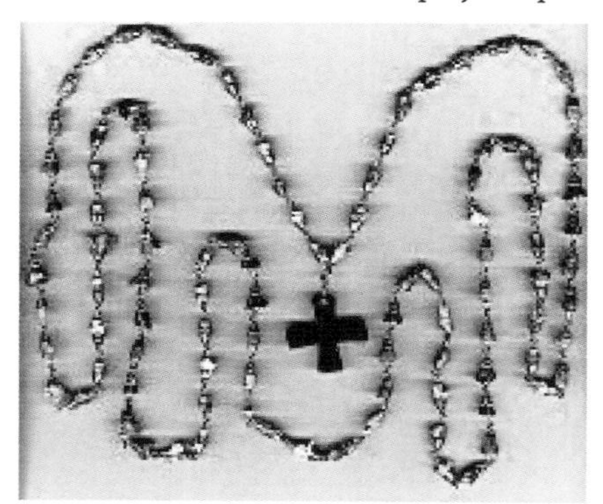

Marian Rosary to honor Pope John Paul II

Bag of beads for prayers throughout the day.

Eastern Orthodox Prayer Ropes or Chatki

About the Marian or Roman Catholic Rosary

THE ROMAN CATHOLIC faith uses prayer counters in many forms: rosary beads, chaplets, rosary rings and rosary bracelets. Praying the rosary is "a form of vocal and mental prayer on the mysteries" of the life of Jesus Christ (Marian Helpers).

A common misconception of the Roman Catholic Rosary is that it is prayed to Mary. Rather, the meditant prays for the intercession of Mary, to strengthen the meditant's prayers.

The most commonly used rosary is the Dominican Rosary with five decades or groups of ten beads, which used to be called 'the corona' or crown. The Our Father, 10 Hail Marys and the Glory Be accompany each decade. A Pray the Rosary Daily brochure is attached as reference in praying the Roman Catholic Rosary (Marian Helpers).

The Traditional Rosary of the Blessed Virgin Mary had 15 decades (now 20), historically referred to as "The Rosary." Now, all forms of the rosary prayed with Mary's intercession are referred to as The Rosary. Chaplets are rosaries that are prayed in honor of saints and religious orders to further a form of devotion (Shaughnessy 1).

Pope John Paul II named 2002 as The Year of the Rosary and created a new set of Mysteries. The Luminous Mysteries focus on significant events in the life of Christ. With the addition of the new mysteries, there are now 20 mysteries upon which to meditate.

Praying the Marian or Roman Catholic Rosary

The rosary invites a time of contemplation, thanksgiving and a sense of forgiveness for our sins and for those of others. Blessings!

Each rosary has a string of prayer beads and a drop. Please refer to the Pray the Rosary Daily brochure (Marion Helpers); whose permission I have to use their materials in my own way.

The drop of the rosary is composed of a crucifix and the five beads hanging from the string of beads. The beads are arranged in a pattern, or series, of a single bead, three beads together, followed by a single bead. This last bead is attached to the centerpiece that belongs to the body of the rosary.

The body of the rosary is the string of beads made up of 54 beads. The beads are arranged in five decades, or groups of 10 beads. A single bead separates each decade. Connecting the drop of the rosary to the body of the rosary is the centerpiece.

The following is merely an attempt to share the time-honored rhythm and practice of praying the rosary. I have numbered the beads and given them names to indicate the flow and order of the prayers. The cross symbols specify the prayers invited as the rosary prayer unfolds.

As the late Pope said:

"Remember, you are free to pray the rosary in any way you wish. It is a private devotion."

Pope John Paul II, Rosarium Virginis Mariae, 2002

Praying the Marion Rosary

THE DROP OF THE ROSARY Crucifix and 5 drop beads: two single beads and a set of three.		
BEAD	**NAME OF BEAD**	**PRAYER**
Begin	The Crucifix	• *Sign of the Cross* • *The Apostles' Creed*
1	Single Drop Bead I	• *Our Father*
2-4	Three Beads	• *Three Hail Marys* • *Glory Be*
5	Single Drop Bead II	• *Meditate on the First Mystery* • *Our Father*

THE BODY OF THE ROSARY 55 beads: 5 decades, 4 single body beads and a fifth single concluding bead or centerpiece.		
BEAD	**NAME OF BEAD**	**PRAYER**
6-15	First Decade	• *Ten Hail Marys* • *Glory Be*
16	Single Body Bead I	• *Meditate on the Second Mystery* • *Our Father*
17-26	Second Decade	• *Ten Hail Marys* • *Glory Be*
27	Single Body Bead II	• *Meditate on the Third Mystery* • *Our Father*
28-37	Third Decade	• *Ten Hail Marys* • *Glory Be*
38	Single Body Bead III	• *Meditate on the Fourth Mystery* • *Our Father*
39-48	Fourth Decade	• *Ten Hail Marys* • *Glory Be*
49	Single Body Bead IV	• *Meditate on the Fifth Mystery* • *Our Father*
50-59	Fifth Decade	• *Ten Hail Marys* • *Glory Be*
60	Centerpiece or Concluding Bead	• *Hail Holy Queen* • *Sign of the Cross*

The Sign of the Cross

In the name of the Father,

- *and of the Son,*
- *and of the Holy Spirit. Amen.*

The Apostles' Creed

I believe in God, the Father almighty,

- *creator of heaven and earth.*

I believe in Jesus Christ, his only Son, our Lord.

- *He was conceived by the power of the Holy Spirit, and born of the Virgin Mary.*
- *He suffered under Pontius Pilate, was crucified, died, and was buried.*
- *He descended to the dead.*
- *On the third day He rose again.*
- *He ascended into heaven, and is seated at the right hand of the Father.*
- *He will come again to judge the living and the dead.*

I believe in the Holy Spirit,

- *the holy Catholic Church,*
- *the communion of saints,*
- *the forgiveness of sins,*
- *the resurrection of the body,*
- *and life everlasting. Amen*

The Our Father

Our Father, who art in heaven,

- *hallowed be Thy Name;*
- *Thy kingdom come,*
- *Thy will be done on earth as it is in heaven.*

Give us this day, our daily bread;

- *and forgive us our trespasses*
- *as we forgive those who trespass against us,*
- *and lead us not unto temptation; but deliver us from evil. Amen.*

The Hail Mary

Hail Mary,
- *full of grace,*
- *the Lord is with thee;*

Blessed art thou among women,
- *and blessed is the fruit of your womb, Jesus.*

Holy Mary, Mother of God,
- *pray for us sinners,*
- *now and at the hour of our death. Amen.*

Glory Be to the Father

Glory be to the Father,
- *and to the Son,*
- *and to the Holy Spirit.*

As it was in the beginning,
- *is now,*
- *and ever shall be,*
- *world without end. Amen.*

Hail, Holy Queen

Hail, Holy Queen,
- *Mother of Mercy,*
- *Our life, our sweetness and our hope,*
- *To thee do we cry,*

Poor banished children of Eve;
- *To thee do we send up our sighs,*
- *mourning and*
- *weeping in this vale of tears;*

Turn, then, most gracious Advocate,
- *thine eyes of mercy towards us,*
- *and after this, our exile,*
- *show unto us the blessed fruit of thy womb, Jesus.*

O clement, O loving, O sweet Virgin Mary!

Concluding Prayers

Leader says:

- *Pray for us, O holy Mother of God.*

All say:

- *That we may be made worthy of the promises of Christ.*

Let us pray (a Final Prayer)

O God,

- *whose only begotten Son,*
- *by His life, death, and resurrection*
- *has purchased for us the rewards of eternal life,*

Grant, we beseech Thee,

- *that meditating upon these mysteries*
- *in the most Holy Rosary of the Blessed Virgin Mary,*
- *we may imitate what they contain, and*
- *obtain what they promise:*
- *through the same Christ our Lord. Amen.*

"Remember, you are free to pray the rosary in any way you wish. It is a private devotion."

Pope John Paul II, Rosarium Virginis Mariae, 2002

Mysteries of the Rosary

The rosary's focus is to meditate on the life of Jesus as captured in the 15 mysteries: five Joyful Mysteries, five Sorrowful Mysteries and five Glorious Mysteries. When saying the rosary, the meditant thinks of one mystery while saying a complete decade of Hail Marys.

The Joyful Mysteries, meditated upon Mondays and Saturdays

1. *The Annunciation*
2. *The Visitation*
3. *The Birth of Jesus*
4. *The Presentation*
5. *The Finding of the Child Jesus in the Temple*

Sorrowful Mysteries, meditated upon Tuesdays and Fridays

1. *The Agony in the Garden*
2. *The Scourging at the Pillar*
3. *The Crowning with Thorns*
4. *The Carrying of the Cross*
5. *The Crucifixion*

The Glorious Mysteries, meditated upon Sundays and Wednesdays

1. *The Resurrection*
2. *The Ascension*
3. *The Descent of the Holy Spirit upon the Apostles*
4. *The Assumption*
5. *The Crowning of Mary as Queen of Heaven*

New Luminous Mysteries created by Pope John Paul II in 2002, declaring 2002 - the Year of the Rosary.

The Luminous Mysteries, meditated upon Thursdays

1. *The Baptism of Christ in the Jordan*
2. *The Wedding Feast at Cana*
3. *The Announcement of the Kingdom*
4. *The Transfiguration*
5. *The Institution of the Eucharist*

About the Eastern Orthodox, Greek and Russian, Prayer Ropes
The Greek and Russian traditions of the Eastern Orthodox faith use the Dominican Marian Rosary and knotted prayer ropes as prayer counters. The Eastern Orthodox prayer rope is called the Chotki, Russian for "prayer rope," and is divided into decades.

The Greek Orthodox prayer ropes have 33, 50 or 100 knots and are called the Komboschini. The Serbian rosary is the Broyanitasa and has 33, 100 or 300 beads. A unique use of the chotki is as a "silent 'breath prayer,' with 'Lord Jesus Christ, Son of the Living God' prayed on inhalation and 'have mercy on me, a sinner' prayer on exhalation" (Davis 1 from Kikolaj, Russian Orthodox Church, Denmark).

Anglican Prayer Beads

MAKING THE ANGLICAN ROSARY

Making the Anglican Rosary

I LEARNED to make Marian Rosaries from Janet Daut. She learned from a rosary guild. She passed on this gift and a relaxed, prayerful approach to making the rosary. It is a blessing and an honor to pass this gift along to you.

As we make rosaries, alone or with others, we pray. Meditative silence, praying the rosary aloud and joyful chatter all accompany the making of the rosary as living prayer. Guided by our own creative sense, the individual and communal nature of prayer and grace are reinforced and honored.

- The purpose is not beauty, but prayer. Beauty is a lovely side effect of many of our prayerful choices. "We hope that God talks to us. We are so busy asking God for things. The purpose of real prayer is to be still enough to allow God to speak to us" (Father Del Provino).
- Making rosaries is an active way of being still for those of us that have trouble keeping still!

Making Your Own Anglican Rosary

The beauty of making a rosary is that it is all yours. It's up to your creative and aesthetic sensibilities. These pages merely offer guidelines as a starting point in your creative process.

- You can buy or make beads or make knots from cord or string.
- Beads can be made of simple wood, plastic, glass, berries, precious and semi-precious stones, precious or common metal, or made from clay that is baked. Any bead with a hole big enough to be strung will serve.
- My children made beautiful beads out of clay. After all these years, these remain as cherished gifts.
- Enjoy!

Materials for the Anglican Rosary

All that is really needed for making an Anglican, or Episcopalian, Rosary are 33 beads, one for each year of Christ's life, a cross (crucifix without the corpus) and a strand of some sort to connect them.

- For simple rosaries, you will need two sizes of beads, big and medium.
- For less simple rosaries, you will need to add small beads so that you have three sizes of beads.

Materials for Simple Rosaries

Prayerful, joyous attitude

- 33 beads
    - 5 big or different beads
    - 4 Cruciform beads
    - 1 Invitatory bead
    - 28 medium-sized beads
- Cross (crucifix without the corpus, or body of Christ)
- String, wire, cord, or floss (approximately 12 inches)
- Cutting implement
    - Pliers if working with wire
    - Scissors if working with string, cord, or floss

Materials for More Elaborate Rosaries

Same as the Materials for Simple Rosaries noted above and:

- 54 small separator beads
    - 24 separator beads (6 between the 7 medium-sized Hail Mary beads x 4 Weeks)
    - 30 separator beads (3 before and after each of the 5 larger cruciform and invitatory beads x 10)
- 2 beading crimps
    - 2 jump rings (1 before and after the invitatory bead)

Anglican Prayer Beads

WORKS CITED

Works Cited and References

A SPECIAL THANKS for the wisdom, knowledge and generosity of David Willing for information about the Anglican faith, Trinity Cathedral volunteer, Miami, FL; Elena Gurri Levis for artistry; Domenico Travano for technical wisdom; Angela Dellostritto, Michael McCartin, Michael Mullane and Steve Lee for their editing .

Bauman, Lynn C. The Anglican Rosary. PRAXIS, Rt. 1, Box 190B, 78606. Telephone, TX: Praxis, 1997.

Benenate, Becky (ed.). In the Heart of The World, Thoughts, Stories and Prayers. NY: MJK Books, 1997.

Davis, Glenwood T. E. One Episcopalian's Rosary. www.members.aol.com/GDCSoul/rosary.htm.

Eastern Christian Supply Co. Prayer Ropes (Komboschoinia or Chotki). www.easternchristian.com/ropes.html.

Elliott, Kristin M. and Seibt, Betty Kay. Holding Your Prayers in Your Hands: Praying the Anglican Rosary. Denton, TX: Open Hands, 1997.

The Episcopal Church. The Book of Common Prayer, NY: The Church Hymnal Corp. and The Seabury Press, 1977.

Geoffrion, Jill Kimberly Hartwell. Praying the Labyrinth. Cleveland, OH: The Pilgrim Press, 1999.

Marian Helpers, Marians of the Immaculate Conception. Pray the Rosary Daily. Stockbridge, MA: Marian Helpers, 1990. Phone: 800-462-7426.

Monty, Father. Praying the Anglican Rosary. www. Praying The Anglican RosarybyFatherMonty.htm.

Our Lady's Rosary Makers. 4611 Poplar Level Road, PO Box 37080, Louisville, KY 40233. Phone: 502-968-1434.

Our Rose Rosary, Rosaries, Chaplets and Jewelry Made with Real Roses. www.ourroserosary.com/jb.htm.

Pope John Paul II. The Rosarium Virginis Mariae, 2002. www.forheavenssake.net/luminous_mysteries.htm.

Provino, D.A. Conversations with the Rt. Rev. Monsignor D.A. Provino, respected Orthodox Catholic priest, Our Lady Theotokas, Hollywood, FL, summer 2003 through March 2004. Phone: 954-920-8201.

Rose, Anne. Holy Islands, Holy Lives, Holy Habits (handout). St. Thomas Episcopal Church, March 2004.

Schultz, O.H.C., Thomas. The Rosary for Episcopalians. Reprinted from the book, Praying by Hand, by M. Basil Pennington, OCSO. NY: HarperCollins, 1992.

Shaughnessy, OSB, STD, Patrick. Twenty-four Rosaries and Chaplets. St. Meinrud, Indiana: Grail Publications, 1954.

Solitaries of DeKoven. Anglican Prayer Bead, A Rosary for Episcopalians. Pamphlet in the Duncan Center Bookstore.

Celtic Blessing*

May you be
lit by the glory of God,
drawn by the light of God,
warmed by the fire of God. ***Amen.***

*Note: Taken from Ann Rose's handouts, Holy Islands, Holy Lives, Holy Habits, St. Thomas Episcopal Church, March 2004.

An Irish Blessing

May there always be work
for your hands to do;

May your purse always hold
a coin or two;

May the sun always shine
on your windowpane;

May a rainbow be certain
to follow each rain;

May the hand of a friend
always be near you

May God fill your heart
with gladness to cheer you.

Each of us can add grace and joy to our world with individual and community prayer. I hope this little book invites even more prayer, grace and joy. *Blessings!*

Margarita Gurri, Ph.D.

Dr. Gurri is a licensed psychologist who for years has educated and motivated leaders and families, military personnel and couples, parents and youth alike. For her it's all about honest, effective communication and strengthening relationships.

With a proven track record as a consultant, international speaker and author, Dr. Gurri's unique approach is tinged with a bit of humor, sprinkled with plenty of anecdotes and brimming with optimism that stem from, not only her keen insight but her personal and professional experiences as well.

Dr. Gurri has 30 years of experience in the field. She earned a Ph. D. in clinical psychology at the University of Kansas and completed post-graduate work at the University of Maryland and Menninger Institute.

Among her numerous affiliations are: American Psychological Association; Association for Applied and Therapeutic Humor; Florida Psychoanalytical Society; Florida Psychological Association; Florida Speakers Association, Latin America and National Speakers Associations; and the Department of Defense Yellow Ribbon Speaker Cadre.

"Faith is simple, not easy."

Made in the USA
Lexington, KY
10 September 2014